Jack Feels Angry

By Adrian Laurent

Copyright © 2021 by Adrian Laurent

All rights reserved. No part of this book may be reproduced or used in any manner without written permission of the copyright owner except for the use of quotations in a book review.

Limit of Liability/Disclaimer of Warranty:
This is a work of fiction. Names, characters, places, and incidents either are the product of the author's imagination or are used fictitiously. Any resemblance to actual persons, living or dead, events, or locales is entirely coincidental.

Although the publisher and the author have made every effort to ensure that the information in this book was correct at press time and while this publication is designed to provide accurate information in regard to the subject matter covered, the publisher and the author assume no responsibility for errors, inaccuracies, omissions, or any other inconsistencies herein and hereby disclaim any liability to any party for any loss, damage, or disruption caused by errors or omissions, whether such errors or omissions result from negligence, accident, or any other cause.

The information in this book is not intended to be used, nor should be used, to diagnose or treat any mental health or medical condition. For diagnosis or treatment of any mental health or medical condition, consult a licensed professional, psychologist or physician. Both the author and publisher of this book are not liable or responsible for any damages or negative consequences from any preparation, treatment, action, application to any person.

ISBN 978-0-473-58760-4 (paperback)
ISBN 978-0-473-58761-1 (epub)

Bradem Press 2021
New Zealand

www.adrianlaurent.com

Jack watched the rain and sighed, "Soggy day!"
"I'll stay inside for now." But what games could he play?
"I'll find my monster truck." So Jack searched high and low.
But couldn't find it anywhere. Did anyone know?

When Jack came across it, his eyes opened wide.
His sister, Jenny, had his truck by the fireside.
He ran over to her and grabbed for his truck.
But Jenny held tight—Jack's out of luck!

Jack grabbed at her fingers. He pulled, and he pried.
His face went beet red. "It's just not fair," he cried.
Jack stopped and remembered feeling angry is OK.
But don't break, hurt or shout. Help the anger go away.

Last time Jack got angry, he counted up to ten.
"It worked so well that time. It might just work again!"
Jack breathed in and out, his face paled to pink.
His thumping heart slowed, and then Jack could think.

"May I take my truck," asked Jack, reaching out.
"No," replied Jenny with a frown and a pout.
He'd asked politely. What else could he do?
Again, his face burned, and his heart raced anew.

Jack went back to try again and thought what he might say.
"Can I have a turn?" He asked. Jenny yelled, "Go away!"
As she gripped it tightly, a wheel fell to the floor.
Jack stamped his feet; he couldn't cope anymore.

"You should be proud," said mum, "for trying hard to stay calm."
"I have a trick you could try that works like a charm."
"When I get angry, I stretch my fingers and toes."
"I stretch as hard as I can, and my anger just… goes."

So Jack spread out his fingers. He stretched, and he breathed.
His heartbeat slowed down; his anger had eased!
"Please give back Jack's truck," Mum calmly said.
"I'm sorry," said Jenny. "I'll find my truck instead."

"Jack, I see you tried," Said Mum, "to make your anger go."
"You should be proud of yourself and the calming tricks you know."
Jack smiled and turned to Jenny. "Let's play trucks together."
And they played until dinner time, out of the stormy weather.